U.K. YEARBOOK

ISBN: 9798745740596

This book gives a fascinating and informative insight into life in the United Kingdom in 1952. It includes everything from the most popular music of the year to the cost of a buying a new house. Additionally, there are chapters covering people in high office, the best-selling films of the year and all the main news and events. Want to know which team won the FA Cup or which British personalities were born in 1952? All this and much more awaits you within.

INDEX

FIRST EDITION

1952

January
M	T	W	T	F	S	S
	1	2	3	4	5	6
7	8	9	10	11	12	13
14	15	16	17	18	19	20
21	22	23	24	25	26	27
28	29	30	31			

◑:4　○:12　◐:20　●:26

February
M	T	W	T	F	S	S
				1	2	3
4	5	6	7	8	9	10
11	12	13	14	15	16	17
18	19	20	21	22	23	24
25	26	27	28	29		

◑:2　○:11　◐:18　●:25

March
M	T	W	T	F	S	S
					1	2
3	4	5	6	7	8	9
10	11	12	13	14	15	16
17	18	19	20	21	22	23
24	25	26	27	28	29	30
31						

◑:3　○:11　◐:19　●:25

April
M	T	W	T	F	S	S
	1	2	3	4	5	6
7	8	9	10	11	12	13
14	15	16	17	18	19	20
21	22	23	24	25	26	27
28	29	30				

◑:2　○:10　◐:17　●:24

May
M	T	W	T	F	S	S
			1	2	3	4
5	6	7	8	9	10	11
12	13	14	15	16	17	18
19	20	21	22	23	24	25
26	27	28	29	30	31	

◑:2　○:9　◐:16　●:23　◑:31

June
M	T	W	T	F	S	S
						1
2	3	4	5	6	7	8
9	10	11	12	13	14	15
16	17	18	19	20	21	22
23	24	25	26	27	28	29
30						

○:8　◐:14　●:22　◑:30

July
M	T	W	T	F	S	S
	1	2	3	4	5	6
7	8	9	10	11	12	13
14	15	16	17	18	19	20
21	22	23	24	25	26	27
28	29	30	31			

○:7　◐:14　●:22　◑:30

August
M	T	W	T	F	S	S
				1	2	3
4	5	6	7	8	9	10
11	12	13	14	15	16	17
18	19	20	21	22	23	24
25	26	27	28	29	30	31

○:5　◐:12　●:20　◑:28

September
M	T	W	T	F	S	S
1	2	3	4	5	6	7
8	9	10	11	12	13	14
15	16	17	18	19	20	21
22	23	24	25	26	27	28
29	30					

○:4　◐:11　●:19　◑:26

October
M	T	W	T	F	S	S
	1	2	3	4	5	
6	7	8	9	10	11	12
13	14	15	16	17	18	19
20	21	22	23	24	25	26
27	28	29	30	31		

○:3　◐:10　●:18　◑:26

November
M	T	W	T	F	S	S
					1	2
3	4	5	6	7	8	9
10	11	12	13	14	15	16
17	18	19	20	21	22	23
24	25	26	27	28	29	30

○:1　◐:9　●:17　◑:24

December
M	T	W	T	F	S	S
1	2	3	4	5	6	7
8	9	10	11	12	13	14
15	16	17	18	19	20	21
22	23	24	25	26	27	28
29	30	31				

○:1　◐:9　●:17　◑:23　○:31

PEOPLE IN HIGH OFFICE

Monarch - King George VI
Reign: 11th December 1936 - 6th February 1952
Predecessor: Edward VIII

Monarch - Queen Elizabeth II
Reign: 6th February 1952 - Present
Heir Apparent: Charles, Prince of Wales

United Kingdom

Prime Minister
Winston Churchill
Conservative Party
26th October 1951 - 5th April 1955

Australia

Canada

United States

Prime Minister
Sir Robert Menzies
Liberal (Coalition)
19th December 1949
- 26th January 1966

Prime Minister
Louis St. Laurent
Liberal Party
15th November 1948
- 21st June 1957

President
Harry S. Truman
Democratic Party
12th April 1945
- 20th January 1953

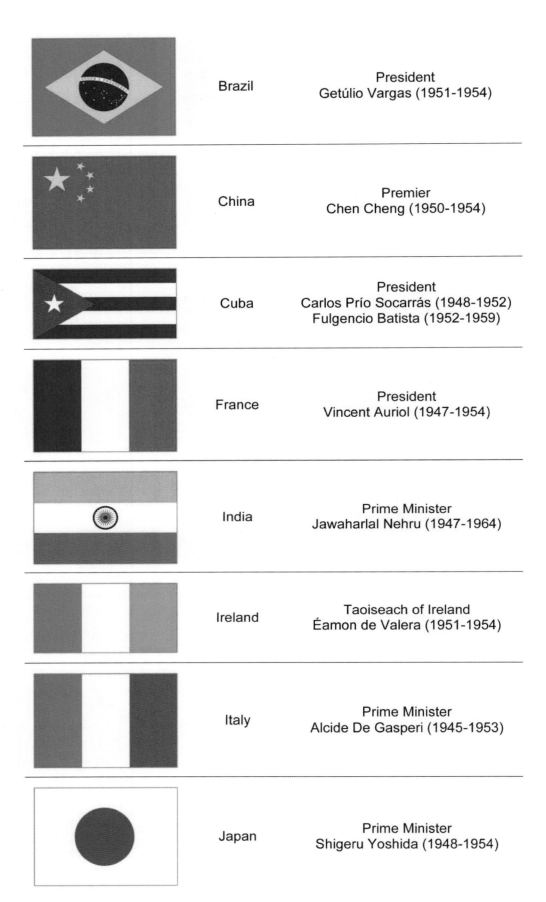

Brazil — President
Getúlio Vargas (1951-1954)

China — Premier
Chen Cheng (1950-1954)

Cuba — President
Carlos Prío Socarrás (1948-1952)
Fulgencio Batista (1952-1959)

France — President
Vincent Auriol (1947-1954)

India — Prime Minister
Jawaharlal Nehru (1947-1964)

Ireland — Taoiseach of Ireland
Éamon de Valera (1951-1954)

Italy — Prime Minister
Alcide De Gasperi (1945-1953)

Japan — Prime Minister
Shigeru Yoshida (1948-1954)

Mexico

President
Miguel Alemán Valdés (1946-1952)
Adolfo Ruiz Cortines (1952-1958)

New Zealand

Prime Minister
Sidney Holland (1949-1957)

Pakistan

Prime Minister
Khawaja Nazimuddin (1951-1953)

Spain

President
Francisco Franco (1938-1973)

South Africa

Prime Minister
Daniel François Malan (1948-1954)

Soviet Union

Communist Party Leader
Joseph Stalin (1922-1953)

Turkey

Prime Minister
Adnan Menderes (1950-1960)

West Germany

Chancellor
Konrad Adenauer (1949-1963)

BRITISH NEWS & EVENTS

JAN

5th	Prime Minister Winston Churchill arrives in the United States for an official visit and talks with President Harry S. Truman.
10th	An Aer Lingus Douglas DC-3 aircraft, on a flight from RAF Northolt, London, to Dublin, crashes in Wales due to powerful down-current of air on the lee side of Snowdon. All twenty passengers and the three crew members are killed.
16th	Sooty, Harry Corbett's glove puppet bear, makes his first appearance on television on the BBC's Talent Night show. *Fun facts: By 1955 Sooty had his own series, The Sooty Show. He was joined in 1957 by his sausage-obsessed squeaky dog friend Sweep, and 1964 by Soo, Sooty's cute panda girlfriend.*
30th	Truce talks aimed at ending the fighting in the Korean War remain deadlocked after weeks of negotiations. *Notes: Nearly 60,000 British combat troops saw action during the war in Korea (1950-1953). Coming from both the regular army and national servicemen, the war resulted in the deaths of some 1,100 British soldiers.*

FEB

1st February: The first TV detector van is demonstrated in front of Postmaster-General, Lord De La Warr, at the King Edward Building in the City of London. Using detection equipment developed at short notice at the radio experimental laboratories of the Post Office in Dollis Hill, London, it is the beginning of a clampdown on the estimated 150,000 British households watching television illegally without a licence. *Photo: The new detector van on show before setting off to track down licence defaulters.*

6th	King George VI dies at Sandringham House aged 56. It is revealed that he had been suffering from lung cancer. He is succeeded by his 25-year-old daughter, Princess Elizabeth, Duchess of Edinburgh, who ascends to the throne as Queen Elizabeth II. The new Queen, on a visit to Kenya at the time of her father's death, returns to London the following day.
14th	The opening ceremony for the 1952 Winter Olympics takes place in Oslo, Norway. *NB: Great Britain and Northern Ireland's only medal came from Jeannette Altwegg who won the gold in the women's figure skating event.*

15th February: The funeral of King George VI takes place at St George's Chapel, Windsor Castle; his body had been lying in state in Westminster Hall since the 11th February. *Photo: King George VI's funeral procession as it passes along Edgware Road towards Paddington Station - from Paddington Station the coffin was taken by train to Windsor for burial.*

21st	After almost thirteen years the National Registration identity card is abolished.
26th	Prime Minister Winston Churchill announces to the house of commons that the United Kingdom has an atomic bomb.

MAR

7th	The first issue of the New Musical Express (NME) newspaper goes on sale. Due to be printed weekly (on a Friday) the papers' cover price is 6d.
31st	Computer scientist Alan Turing is convicted of "gross indecency" after admitting to a consensual homosexual relationship in Regina v. Turing and Murray. He consents to undergo oestrogen treatment (designed to reduce his libido) to avoid imprisonment.

APR

5th In the 106th Grand National, jockey Arthur Thompson and trainer Neville Crump combine for their second win in the race with Teal, winning at odds of 100/7. *NB: Thompson and Crump had previously won the steeplechase in 1948 with 50/1 shot Sheila's Cottage.*

12th Reindeer are reintroduced to the Cairngorms by Mikel Utsi, a Swedish Sami man who saw potential to bring reindeer back to Scotland. *NB: Over 60 years later the herd has gone from strength to strength and now stands at over 150 animals.*

29th Queen Elizabeth II grants the University of Southampton a Royal Charter, the first to be given to a university during her reign, enabling it to award degrees. Six faculties are created: Arts, Science, Engineering, Economics, Education and Law.

MAY

2nd A British Overseas Airways Corporation (BOAC) de Havilland Comet, carrying passengers from London to Johannesburg, South Africa, becomes the first jet aircraft to enter commercial service.

3rd Newcastle United win the FA Cup for a record fifth time with a 1-0 win over Arsenal at Wembley Stadium. The only goal of the game is scored by Chilean-born forward George Robledo, the first foreign player to score in an FA Cup final.

7th British radar engineer Geoffrey Dummer introduces the concept of the integrated circuit (microchip) at a tech conference in Washington, DC.

8th The 5th British Film and Television Awards (BAFTAS), honouring the best in film from 1951, are held at the Odeon Theatre, Marble Arch, London: The Lavender Hill Mob wins the award for the Best British Film, whilst the Best Film from any Source is won by La Ronde.

18th Ann Davison departs Plymouth in her 23-foot wooden sloop Felicity Ann in an attempt to become the first woman to single-handedly sail the Atlantic Ocean. Relatively inexperienced she is met with many challenges but overcomes them all and eventually makes it to New York on the 23rd November 1953.

21st Eastcastle Street robbery: A post office van is held up in the West End of London and £287,000 (worth over £9 million in 2020) is stolen. At the time it is Britain's largest post-war robbery for which, despite the involvement of over 1,000 police officers, no one is ever caught.

JUN

1st A one shilling charge is introduced for prescription drugs dispensed under the National Health Service.

5th Fred Trueman makes his Test cricket debut against India at Headingley. *Fun facts: Trueman is generally acknowledged to have been one of the greatest bowlers in the history of cricket and was the first bowler to take 300 wickets in a Test career. He was awarded the OBE in the 1989 for services to cricket, and was inducted into the ICC Cricket Hall of Fame in 2009.*

14th Jim Peters sets a world record time of 2h:20m:42.2s in the Polytechnic Marathon at Windsor. *Fun facts: Peters would go on to break the world record three more times and become the first to set a time under 2h:20m in 1953.*

6th July: After nearly a century of service the tram makes its final appearance in London. The very last tram to rumble along the capital's streets arrives at south-east London's New Cross depot in the early hours of the 6th July, its journey time extended by almost three hours by crowds of cheering Londoners. Driven by John Cliff, deputy chairman of London Transport Executive, conductors punched souvenir tickets and enthusiasts drove or cycled alongside the tram. *Photo: A tram outside Embankment Underground Station on the last day of operation.*

19th	The opening ceremony for the 1952 Summer Olympics takes place in Helsinki, Finland. *NB: Great Britain and Northern Ireland win 11 medals; 1 gold (equestrian, jumping team competition), 2 silver and 8 bronze.*

AUG

15th	Lynmouth Flood: Thirty-four people are killed in a flood at Lynmouth in Devon after nine inches of rainfall in the space of 24 hours. More than 100 buildings are destroyed or seriously damaged, leaving 420 people homeless. *Notes: A BBC investigation in 2001 fuelled speculation that the flood was caused by secret cloud seeding experiments carried out by the RAF; the MOD responded by declaring it knew nothing of these so-called experiments.*

SEP

6th	A prototype de Havilland DH.110 jet fighter crashes during an aerial display at the Farnborough Airshow in Hampshire. The jet disintegrates mid-air during an aerobatic manoeuvre causing the death of pilot John Derry and onboard flight test observer Anthony Richards. Debris from the aircraft falls onto the crowd of spectators, killing 29 people and injuring 60.

19th | British film star Charlie Chaplin, sailing to England with his family for the premiere of his film Limelight (London, 16th October), is told that he will be refused re-entry to the United States until he has been investigated by the U.S. Immigration Service (because of his perceived communist sympathies). *Follow up: When Chaplin arrives in the U.K., he quickly realises it will be impossible for him to return to the U.S., his home of over 40 years. He decides to move to and settle in Switzerland. He did eventually return to the U.S. in 1972 to accept a Special Academy Award (for which he received a 12-minute standing ovation, the longest in Oscar history).*

29th | The Manchester Guardian (now just The Guardian) prints news, rather than advertisements, on its front page for the first time. The change significantly boosts circulation.

OCT

3rd October: Operation Hurricane: The U.K. explodes its first atomic bomb in a lagoon in the Monte Bello Islands off the Pilbara coast of north-western Australia. *NB: The success of Operation Hurricane sees Britain become the third nuclear power after the United States and the Soviet Union. Photo: Thousands of tons of water, mud and sand blacken the gigantic fireball that results from the explosion of Britain's first atom bomb.*

3rd | The Minister of Food, Major Gwilym Lloyd-George, announces during a speech in Newcastle that tea rationing, in force since January 1940, will end on the 5th October.

6th | Agatha Christie's play The Mousetrap opens in London's West End. *NB: It is the longest running play in history having run continuously until the 16th March 2020 (when performances were discontinued due to the COVID-19 pandemic).*

OCT

8th	A three-train collision at Harrow and Wealdstone station in Wealdstone, Middlesex (now Greater London) during the morning rush hour kills 112 people and injures 340. *NB: It remains today Britain's worst peacetime rail crash.*
19th	John Bamford, aged 15, rescues his two younger brothers from their upstairs bedroom when a fire breaks out during the night at their home in Newthorpe, near Eastwood in Nottinghamshire. *Follow up: Bamford took four months to recover from the injuries he sustained during the fire. His bravery was rewarded when, in December 1952, he became the youngest person to be awarded the George Cross.*

NOV

	The College of General Practitioners, later to become the Royal College of General Practitioners (RCGP), is founded.
14th	The first regular U.K. singles chart is published by the New Musical Express. American crooner Al Martino takes the inaugural Official Singles Chart No.1 with his track "Here In My Heart". He would hold onto the top spot for nine consecutive weeks.
29th	Scotland's first GPO pillar box of the reign of Queen Elizabeth II is erected on the Inch housing estate in Edinburgh. The EIIR box quickly causes controversy and is defaced with tar within 36 hours. *Notes: The problem with the box was that the Tudor Queen Elizabeth I had never ruled over Scotland, therefore the suggestion that there could be a Queen Elizabeth II was considered grossly inaccurate and unacceptable to many Scots. Follow up: On the 12th February 1953, the three-month-old Inch post box was completely blown apart by a gelignite bomb. A brand-new pillar box appeared shortly after with no sign of EIIR. To avoid further troubles, after 1953 new post boxes placed in Scotland carried only the Crown of Scotland image rather than the EIIR cypher.*

DEC

5th	A thick layer of smog blankets London (4th - 9th December) causing transport chaos and in excess of 4,000 deaths. Additionally, more than 100,000 people are made ill by the smog, thought to be the worst air pollution event in the history of the United Kingdom. *NB: The Great Smog of 1952 led to several changes in practices and regulations, including the Clean Air Act 1956.*
10th	British chemists Archer Martin and Richard Synge are awarded the Nobel Prize in Chemistry "for their invention of partition chromatography".
12th	The children's television series Flower Pot Men debuts on BBC television.
25th	The Queen gives her first Christmas message to the Commonwealth of Nations from her study at Sandringham House. *Fun facts: The tradition of the Royal Christmas Message began in 1932 with a radio broadcast by King George V on the BBC's Empire Service. The Queens 1957 Christmas Message was the first to be broadcast on television.*
30th	An RAF Avro Lancaster bomber crashes in Luqa, Malta after an engine failure. Three of the four crew members and a civilian on the ground are killed.

Worldwide News & Events

1. 26th January: Hundreds of buildings are deliberately set ablaze in downtown Cairo following the killing of Egyptian policemen by British Army troops stationed along the Suez Canal Zone.
2. 10th February: The Congress Party of India, led by Jawaharlal Nehru, wins an outright victory in the country's first general election.
3. 14th - 25th February: The Winter Olympics are held in Oslo, Norway; 694 athletes from 30 countries compete at the games.
4. 18th February: Greece and Turkey join the North Atlantic Treaty Organisation (NATO).
5. 21st February: The 9th Golden Globe Awards, honouring the best in film for 1951, are held at Ciro's nightclub in West Hollywood, California. The winners include the film A Place in the Sun, Fredric March and Jane Wyman.
6. 26th February: Vincent Massey is sworn in as the first Canadian-born Governor General of Canada.
7. 10th March: General Fulgencio Batista stages a coup in Cuba, taking over Havana and the Presidential Palace.
8. 15th - 16th March: Over a 24-hour period a record 73 inches of rain falls on Reunion Island in the Indian Ocean.
9. 20th March: The 24th Academy Awards, honouring the best in film for 1951, are held at RKO Pantages Theatre in Hollywood, California. Hosted by Danny Kaye, the winners include the film An American in Paris, Humphrey Bogart and Vivian Leigh.
10. 21st March: The last executions to be carried out in the Netherlands take place at Waalsdorpervlakte (SS officers Andries Jan Pieters and Artur Albrecht).
11. 21st March: Alan Freed presents the Moondog Coronation Ball, the world's first major rock and roll concert, at the Cleveland Arena in Ohio. 20,000 fans turn up to the arena which has a capacity of just 10,000. The frustrated crowd storm the arena but police quickly move in and stop the show.
12. 21st March: Tornadoes ravage the Southern United States (primarily the lower Mississippi River Valley) leaving 209 dead.
13. 27th March: A package addressed to West German Chancellor Konrad Adenauer explodes killing Bavarian police officer Karl Reichert. *Follow up: Later investigations reveal that the mastermind behind the assassination attempt is Menachem Begin, who would later become the Prime Minister of Israel.*
14. 30th March: The 6th Annual Tony Awards are presented at the Waldorf-Astoria Grand Ballroom in New York City. The winners include The Fourposter (most Outstanding Play), and The King and I (most Outstanding Musical).
15. 5th April: During a severe storm in the area of the West Ice, east of Greenland, 78 men on 5 Norwegian seal hunting vessels vanish without a trace.
16. 11th April: Bolivian National Revolution: Hugo Ballivián's government is overthrown by Hernán Siles Zuazo and his MNR Party, aided by defectors from the armed forces.
17. 15th April: The American Boeing B-52 Stratofortress strategic bomber flies for the first time. *Notes: The B-52 is capable of carrying up to 31,750kg of weapons and has a typical combat range of more than 8,800 miles. It is the longest-serving combat aircraft in the world and is expected to serve into the 2050's.*

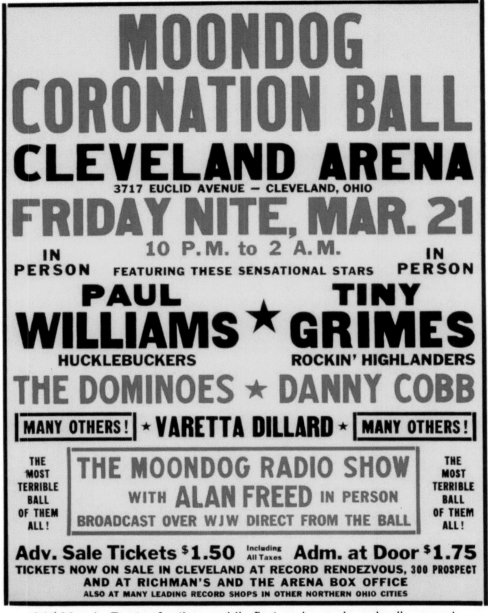

21st March: Poster for the world's first major rock and roll concert.

18. | 28th April: The Treaty of San Francisco (signed by 49 nations on the 8th September 1951) goes into effect formally re-establishing peaceful relations between Japan and the Allied Powers on behalf of the United Nations.

19. | 28th April: Dwight D. Eisenhower resigns as Supreme Commander of NATO to run for President of the United States.

20. | 3rd May: Pilot William P. Benedict and his co-pilot Joseph O. Fletcher, along with scientist Albert P. Crary, become the first Americans to fly to, land and set foot on the geographic North Pole.

21. | 5th May: The Pulitzer Prize for Fiction is awarded to Herman Wouk for his novel The Caine Mutiny.

22. | 10th May: At the 5th Cannes Film Festival, Othello, directed by Orson Welles, and Two Cents Worth of Hope, directed by Renato Castellani, are jointly awarded the Grand Prix du Festival International du Film (now the Palme d'Or).

23.	28th May: For the first time all women in Greece are granted the right to vote and stand in elections.
24.	13th June: The Catalina affair: Soviet MiG-15 fighter planes shoot down a Swedish Air Force Douglas DC-3, carrying out signals intelligence gathering operations over the Baltic Sea, killing all 8 crew. Three days later they shoot down a Catalina flying boat involved in the search and rescue operation for the missing DC-3. The Catalina's crew of five are all rescued.
25.	14th June: In the United States the keel is laid for the world's first operational nuclear-powered submarine, USS Nautilus, at General Dynamics' Electric Boat Division in Groton, Connecticut.
26.	14th June: Myxomatosis is introduced to Europe on the French estate of Dr. Paul-Félix Armand-Delille; his intention was to eradicate the rabbits on his property but the disease quickly spreads throughout Western Europe.
27.	15th June: The English-language translation of Anne Frank's "The Diary of a Young Girl" is reviewed by Meyer Levin in the New York Times. This leads to a rapid increase in sales with print run after print run selling out.
28.	26th June: The Defiance Campaign is launched in South Africa. It is the largest scale non-violent resistance ever seen in the country and the first campaign pursued jointly by all racial groups under the leadership of the ANC and the South African Indian Congress (SAIC).
29.	28th June: The First Miss Universe is held in Long Beach, California, and is won by Armi Kuusela from Finland.
30.	3rd July: In the United States Dr. Forest Dewey Dodrill becomes the first surgeon to use a mechanical heart pump on a patient (41-year-old Henry Opitek).

31. 3rd July: On her maiden voyage the ocean liner SS United States crosses the Atlantic and breaks the eastbound transatlantic speed record (held by the British liner RMS Queen Mary for the previous 14 years) by more than 10 hours. On her return voyage the United States also breaks the westbound transatlantic speed record. *NB: The ship is still today the fastest ocean liner to cross the Atlantic in either direction. Photo: Cheering crowds greet the SS United States in Southampton, England, after her record-breaking maiden voyage.*

32.	19th July - 3rd August: The 1952 Summer Olympics are held in Helsinki, Finland. A total of 4,955 athletes from 69 counties compete in 149 events, with the Soviet Union and Israel doing so for the first time. The United States win the most medals with 76, the Soviet Union come in second with 71, and the host nation eighth with 22.
33.	19th July: Several alleged UFOs are tracked on multiple radars over Washington D.C. during the weekend of the 19th and 20th July. Jets scramble on several occasions but the objects disappear, only to return after the jets run low on fuel and leave the area. *Notes: The sightings were part of a series of unidentified flying object reports between the 12th and 29th July 1952. The U.S. Air Force's official explanation stated that the visual sightings could have been stars or meteors, and that the unknown radar targets could be explained by temperature inversion. This explanation was not accepted by everyone and fuelled some of the earliest conspiracy theories of a government plot to hide evidence of alien life.*
34.	19th July: Fausto Coppi of Italy wins the 39th Tour de France.
35.	23rd July: The Free Officers, led by Muhammad Naguib and Gamal Abdel Nasser, stage a military coup in Egypt.
36.	26th July: King Farouk I of Egypt is forced to abdicate in favour of his baby son, Ahmed Fuad, who is proclaimed King Fuad II.
37.	25th July: Puerto Rico becomes a self-governing commonwealth of the United States.
38.	26th July: Argentine First Lady Eva Peron dies of cancer at the age of 33.
39.	27th July: Having already won 5,000m and 10,000m gold medals, Czech star Emil Zátopek claims rare Olympic treble after a last-minute decision to compete in the first marathon of his life at the Helsinki Games; he completes the feat in an Olympic record time of 2h 23m 3.2s.
40.	1st August: A massive volcanic eruption on San Benedicto Island in the Pacific Ocean brings about the extinction of the San Benedicto rock wren.
41.	3rd August: With two races still to go, Italian Scuderia Ferrari driver Alberto Ascari clinches the Formula 1 World Drivers Championship at the Nürburgring in Germany.
42.	4th August: African-American mob boss Theodore Roe, nicknamed "Robinhood" because of his philanthropy among the poor in Chicago, Illinois, is murdered by the crew of Sam Giancana.
43.	5th August: The Treaty of Taipei between Japan and the Republic of China goes into effect, officially ending the Second Sino-Japanese War (1937-1945).
44.	11th August: The Jordanian Parliament forces King Talal of Jordan to abdicate due to mental illness; he is succeeded by his son Hussein.
45.	12th August: Night of the Murdered Poets: Thirteen Soviet Jews are executed at Lubyanka Prison in Moscow after being accused of espionage, treason and a number of other crimes. *Follow up: On the 22nd November 1955, the Military Collegium of the Supreme Court of the USSR determined that there was "no substance to the charges" against them and the case was closed.*
46.	13th August: Japan joins the IMF; 14th August: Germany joins the IMF.
47.	20th August - 12th September: The 13th Venice International Film Festival is held; Forbidden Games, directed by René Clément, wins the Golden Lion (best film).
48.	26th August: Mother Teresa opens the "Kalighat Home for the Dying Destitutes" in Calcutta, India.
49.	29th August: Pianist David Tudor premieres John Cage's three-movement composition 4'33" at the Maverick Concert Hall in Woodstock, New York. Composed for any instrument (or combination of instruments) the score instructs performers not to play their instruments for the entire duration of the piece.

50. | 2nd September: In the United States Dr. C. Walton Lillehei and Dr. F. John Lewis perform the world's first successful open-heart operation at the University of Minnesota.

51. | 6th September: The first television station in Canada, CBC's CBFT in Montreal, Quebec, begins bilingual broadcasting.

52. | 8th September: Ernest Hemingway's last major work of fiction "The Old Man and the Sea" is published. Printed in its entirety in Life Magazine, the novella sparks a buying frenzy and just over five million copies of the magazine are sold in just two days. *NB: The short story is awarded the Pulitzer Prize for Fiction in 1953.*

53. | 10th September: The Reparations Agreement between Israel and the Federal Republic of Germany is signed in Luxembourg (effective 27th March 1953). West Germany agrees to pay Israel a sum of 3 billion marks over the next fourteen years.

54. 23rd September: Undefeated Rocky Marciano KOs defending champion Jersey Joe Walcott in the 13th round at Municipal Stadium in Philadelphia to take the NBA, NYSAC, The Ring, and lineal heavyweight boxing titles. *Fun fact: Marciano is the only world heavyweight champion to have finished his career undefeated (49-0, 1947-1956). Photo: Marciano KOs Jersey Joe Walcott for the heavyweight title.*

55. | 24th September: The fast-food restaurant chain KFC opens its first franchise in Salt Lake City, Utah.

56. | 30th September: The Cinerama widescreen film system, developed by Fred Waller, debuts with the movie This Is Cinerama, at the Broadway Theatre in New York City.

57.	7th October: Inventors Norman Joseph Woodland and Bernard Silver are granted a U.S. patent for the barcode.
58.	9th October: In New York construction is completed on the $65 million Manhattan headquarters of the United Nations.
59.	11th - 15th October: The Republic of China seizes Nanri Island from the People's Republic of China.
60.	15th October: Harper & Brothers publish E. B. White's classic children's novel Charlotte's Web.
61.	19th October: Frenchman Alain Bombard departs the Canary Islands on his solitary journey across the Atlantic Ocean to test his theory that a shipwrecked person could survive. Sailing a Zodiac inflatable boat, and taking only a sextant and almost no provisions, he successfully reaches Barbados 65 days later having lost some 25kg (55lbs) in weight.
62.	31st October: With an average coast-to-coast precipitation of 0.54 inches, October 1952 is the driest month over the contiguous United States since records began in 1886 (the second-driest, November 1917, averaged 0.95 inches).
63.	1st November: Operation Ivy (United States): The first successful full-scale test of a multi-megaton thermonuclear weapon (hydrogen bomb), codenamed Mike, takes place at Eniwetok Atoll in the central Pacific Ocean. With a yield of 10.4 megatons, it is almost 500 times more explosive than the bomb dropped on Nagasaki during World War II.

64. 4th November: Republican Dwight D. Eisenhower wins a landslide victory in the 1952 U.S. Presidential Election. Republicans also win control of both houses of Congress. *Fun fact: This election was the first in which a computer (the UNIVAC I) was used to predict the results; it came within 3.5% of Eisenhower's popular vote tally, and four votes off his electoral vote total. Photo: Dwight D. Eisenhower and running mate Richard M. Nixon celebrate their election win.*

65.   4th November: A 9.0Mw earthquake hits the Kamchatka Peninsula of the Soviet Union with a maximum Mercalli intensity of XI (Extreme). The earthquake, the most powerful in Russian history, triggers a major tsunami which results in the deaths of over 2,300 people.

66. 19th November: U.S. Air Force test pilot Captain James Slade Nash sets a world aircraft speed record of 698mph in a North American F-86D Sabre fighter aircraft. *Photo: Captain Nash in his record setting F-86D Sabre Jet.*

67.   19th November: Spain is admitted to UNESCO by a vote of 44 to 4.
68.   20th November: The first official commercial intercontinental flight over the Artic lands in Los Angeles having flown some 5,852 miles from Copenhagen, Denmark. The Douglas Super DC-6 took 25 hours 25 minutes to cover the distance, stopping in Sondre Stromfjord, Greenland, and Winnipeg, Canada on the way.
69.   29th November: President-elect Eisenhower fulfills a political campaign promise and travels to Korea to find out what can be done to end the conflict.
70.   1st December: Adolfo Ruiz Cortines takes office as President of Mexico.
71.   8th December: Yitzhak Ben-Zwi is elected as the second president of Israel; he assumes office on the 16th December.
72.   20th December: An Air Force C-124 Globemaster II military transport aircraft crashes near Moses Lake, Washington; of the 115 people on board, 87 are killed.
73.   27th December: In the U.S., thirteen-year-old Jimmy Boyd's record "I Saw Mommy Kissing Santa Claus" reaches No.1 on the Billboard Singles Chart; the record goes on to sell in excess of 3 million copies.
74.   29th December: The Sonotone 1010 hearing aid is introduced and becomes the very first commercial product to use a transistor.
75.   31st December: At the 41st Davis Cup Australia beats the USA 4-1 in Adelaide.

BIRTHS

British Personalities

BORN IN 1952

Kim Hartman
b. 11th January 1952

Actress best known for her role as Private Helga Geerhart in the sitcom 'Allo 'Allo!

Tim Healy
b. 29th January 1952

Actor - Auf Wiedersehen, Pet; Benidorm; Still Open All Hours.

Simon MacCorkindale
b. 12th February 1952
d. 14th October 2010
Actor, film director, writer and producer.

Simon Woodroffe, OBE
b. 14th February 1952

Motivational speaker and entrepreneur who started the YO! Sushi chain in 1997.

Martin O'Neill, OBE
b. 1st March 1952

Football manager and player who was capped 64 times for Northern Ireland.

John Altman
b. 2nd March 1952

Actor and singer perhaps best known for playing Nick Cotton in EastEnders.

Sir **Philip Green**
b. 15th March 1952

Businessman and former chairman of the Arcadia Group.

Gary Moore
b. 4th April 1952
d. 6th February 2011
Blues/rock guitarist, singer and songwriter.

Eric Pickles, Baron Pickles, Kt, PC
b. 20th April 1952

Conservative politician who served as an MP for Brentwood and Ongar (1992-2017).

Allan Wells, MBE
b. 3rd May 1952

Sprinter who won the 100m gold medal at the 1980 Moscow Summer Olympics.

Michael Barrymore
b. 4th May 1952

Actor, comedian and television game show presenter.

Frances Fisher
b. 11th May 1952

British-born American actress.

David Byrne
b. 14th May 1952

Talking Heads singer, songwriter, record producer, actor, writer and filmmaker.

Liam Neeson, OBE
b. 7th June 1952

Northern Irish actor who holds Irish, British, and American citizenship.

Alastair Stewart, OBE
b. 22nd June 1952

Journalist and newscaster.

Gordon McQueen
b. 26th June 1952

Footballer who was capped 30 times for Scotland.

Dame **Hilary Mantel**, DBE, FRSL
b. 6th July 1952

Writer who has been awarded the Booker Prize twice.

John Kettley
b. 11th July 1952

Freelance weatherman.

Liz Mitchell
b. 12th July 1952

Vocalist best known as one of the original singers of the disco/reggae band Boney M.

Joe Johnson
b. 29th July 1952

Snooker player best known for winning the 1986 World Championship.

Alexei Sayle
b. 7th August 1952

Stand-up comedian, actor, TV presenter, author and former recording artist.

Charlie Whiting
b. 12th August 1952
d. 14th March 2019
Formula 1 Race Director, Safety Delegate, and head of the F1 Technical Department.

John Emburey
b. 20th August 1952

Cricketer and coach who briefly served as
England Test captain in 1988.

Joe Strummer
b. 21st August 1952
d. 22nd December 2002
Musician, singer, songwriter, composer,
actor and radio host (The Clash).

Dave Stewart
b. 9th September 1952

Musician, songwriter and record producer
(Eurythmics).

Jack Wild
b. 30th September 1952
d. 1st March 2006
Actor and singer best known for his debut
role as the Artful Dodger in Oliver! (1968).

Sharon Osbourne
b. 9th October 1952

British-American television personality,
entertainment manager and author.

Sir **Andrew Motion**, FRSL
b. 26th October 1952

Poet, novelist and biographer who was
Poet Laureate from 1999 to 2009.

Delroy Lindo
b. 18th November 1952

British-American actor of film, stage and television.

William Henry "Dusty" Hare, MBE
b. 29th November 1952

International England rugby union footballer.

Mel Smith
b. 3rd December 1952
d. 19th July 2013
Comedian and film director.

Clive Anderson
b. 10th December 1952

Television and radio presenter, comedy writer and former barrister.

John Francome, MBE
b. 13th December 1952

National Hunt Champion Jockey, television pundit and author.

Jenny Agutter, OBE
b. 20th December 1952

Film, stage and television actress.

Notable British Deaths

5th Jan	Victor Alexander John Hope, 2nd Marquess of Linlithgow, KG, KT, GCSI, GCIE, OBE, TD, PC, FRSE (b. 24th September 1887 - d. 5th January 1952) - Unionist politician, agriculturalist and colonial administrator who served as Governor-General and Viceroy of India from 1936 to 1943.
6th Feb	George VI (b. Albert Frederick Arthur George; 14th December 1895 - d. 6th February 1952) - King of the United Kingdom and the Dominions of the British Commonwealth from the 11th December 1936 until his death. He was also concurrently the last emperor of India until August 1947, when the British Raj was dissolved.
10th Feb	Henry Drysdale Dakin, FRS (b. 12th March 1880 - d. 10th February 1952) – Chemist who in 1905 was one of the first scientists to successfully synthesise adrenaline in the laboratory.
13th Feb	Elizabeth MacKintosh (b. 25th July 1896 - d. 13th February 1952) - Scottish author who wrote under the pseudonym Josephine Tey.
19th Feb	Percy Reginald Lawrence-Grant (b. 30th October 1870 - d. 19th February 1952) - Actor known for his supporting roles in films such as Shanghai Express (1932), The Mask of Fu Manchu (1932) and Son of Frankenstein (1939).
4th Mar	Sir Charles Scott Sherrington, OM, PRS, FRCP, FRCS (b. 27th November 1857 - d. 4th March 1952) - Neurophysiologist, histologist, bacteriologist, pathologist, Nobel laureate and president of the Royal Society from 1920 to 1925.
15th Mar	Nevil Vincent Sidgwick, FRS (b. 8th May 1873 - d. 15th March 1952) - Theoretical chemist who made significant contributions to the theory of valency and chemical bonding.
5th Apr	Charles Benjamin Collett, OBE (b. 10th September 1871 - d. 5th April 1952) - Chief Mechanical Engineer of the Great Western Railway from 1922 to 1941.
21st Apr	Leslie James Banks, CBE (b. 9th June 1890 - d. 21st April 1952) - Stage and screen actor, director and producer, now best remembered for playing gruff, menacing characters in black-and-white films of the 1930s and 1940s.
21st Apr	Sir Richard Stafford Cripps, CH, QC, FRS (b. 24th April 1889 - d. 21st April 1952) - Labour Party politician, barrister and diplomat who served as Chancellor of the Exchequer between 1947 and 1950.
16th May	Alec Hearne (b. 22nd July 1863 - d. 16th May 1952) - Cricketer who played for Kent County Cricket Club between 1884 and 1906, and made one Test match appearance for England in 1892.
7th Jun	Sir Charles Otto Desmond MacCarthy, FRSL (b. 20th May 1877 - d. 7th June 1952) - Writer and the foremost literary and dramatic critic of his day.
25th Jun	Alexander Ross (b. 15th September 1879 - d. 25th June 1952) - Scottish professional golfer who won the 1907 U.S. Open.
22nd Aug	Albert Mansbridge, CH (b. 10th January 1876 - d. 22nd August 1952) - Educator who was one of the pioneers of adult education in Britain. He is best known for his part in co-founding the Workers' Educational Association (WEA) in England in 1903, serving as its first secretary until 1915.
6th Sep	Gertrude Lawrence (b. 4th July 1898 - d. 6th September 1952) - Actress, singer, dancer and musical comedy performer best known for her stage appearances on the West End and Broadway.

16th Sep	Matilda Alice Powles (b. 13th May 1864 - d. 16th September 1952) - Music hall performer who adopted the stage name Vesta Tilley and became one of the best-known male impersonators of her era.
22nd Sep	Major General John Hay Beith, CBE, MC (b. 17th April 1876 - d. 22nd September 1952) - Schoolmaster and soldier best remembered as a novelist, playwright, essayist and historian who wrote under the pen name Ian Hay.
29th Sep	John Rhodes Cobb (b. 2nd December 1899 - d. 29th September 1952) - Racing motorist who held the World Land Speed Record three times (1938, 1939 and 1947). He was killed whilst piloting a jet powered speedboat attempting to break the World Water Speed Record on Loch Ness in Scotland.
30th Sep	Waldorf Astor, 2nd Viscount Astor, DL (b. 19th May 1879 - d. 30th September 1952) - American-born English politician and newspaper proprietor.
20th Oct	Arthur Basil Radford (b. 25th June 1897 - d. 20th October 1952) - Character actor who featured in many British films of the 1930s and 1940s.
28th Oct	William Morris Hughes, CH, KC (b. 25th September 1862 - d. 28th October 1952) - Welsh-descended politician who served as the 7th Prime Minister of Australia from 1915 to 1923.
28th Nov	Rosa Lewis (b. 26th September 1867 - d. 28th November 1952) - Cook and owner of The Cavendish Hotel in London. Known as the "Queen of Cooks", her culinary skills were highly prized by Edward VII.

8th December: Charles Herbert Lightoller, DSC & Bar, RD, RNR (b. 30th March 1874 - d. 8th December 1952) - Naval officer who was the most senior member of the crew to survive the Titanic disaster. As the officer in charge of loading passengers into lifeboats on the port side, Lightoller strictly enforced the women and children only protocol, not allowing any male passengers to board the lifeboats unless they were needed as auxiliary seamen.

In World War I Lightoller served as a lieutenant-commander in the Royal Navy and was twice decorated for gallantry. During World War II, in retirement, he provided and sailed one of the "little ships" that played a part in the Dunkirk evacuation. Rather than allow his motor yacht to be requisitioned by the Admiralty, he sailed the vessel to Dunkirk personally and repatriated 127 British servicemen.

15th Dec	Sir William Goscombe John, RA (b. 21st February 1860 - d. 15th December 1952) - Prolific Welsh sculptor known for his many public memorials.
19th Dec	Joseph William Henry Makepeace (b. 22nd August 1881 - d. 19th December 1952) - Cricketer and footballer who appeared for his country four times playing each sport. He is one of just 12 English double internationals.

POPULAR MUSIC

Al Martino	No.1	Here In My Heart
Vera Lynn	No.2	Auf Wiederseh'n Sweetheart
Nat King Cole	No.3	Unforgettable
Teresa Brewer	No.4	Longing For You
Vera Lynn	No.5	The Homing Waltz
Guy Mitchell	No.6	There's Always Room At Our House
Jo Stafford	No.7	Ay-Round The Corner
Mario Lanza	No.8	The Loveliest Night Of The Year
Rosemary Clooney	No.9	Half As Much
Jo Stafford	No.10	You Belong To Me

Notes: The official U.K. pop chart based on record sales did not start until the 14th November 1952, and was first published in New Musical Express magazine. For earlier in 1952 the weekly pop chart, based on the sales of sheet music published by Melody Maker and broadcast by Radio Luxembourg, has been used; sheet music outsold records in the U.K. in the early 1950s.

Al Martino
Here In My Heart

Label:	**Written by:**	**Length:**
Capitol Records	Borrelli / Levinson / Genaro	3 mins 11 secs

Al Martino (b. Jasper Cini; 7th October 1927 - d. 13th October 2009) was a singer and actor. He had his greatest success as a singer between the early 1950s and mid-1970s, being described as "one of the great Italian American pop crooners". He also became well known as an actor, particularly for his role as singer Johnny Fontane in The Godfather. "Here In My Heart" was the first ever No.1 in the U.K. Singles Charts, remaining in the top position for nine weeks.

Vera Lynn
Auf Wiederseh'n Sweetheart

Label:	**Written by:**	**Length:**
Decca	Storch / Parsons	2 mins 38 secs

Dame **Vera Margaret Lynn**, CH, DBE, OStJ (née Welch; b. 20th March 1917 - d. 18th June 2020) was a singer, songwriter and actress whose musical recordings and performances were enormously popular during World War II. "Auf Wiederseh'n Sweetheart", which featured accompaniment by Soldiers and Airmen of HM Forces and the Johnny Johnston Singers, was the first song recorded by a foreign artist to make it to No.1 on the U.S. Billboard charts (1952).

3 Nat King Cole
Unforgettable

Label:	Written by:	Length:
Capitol Records	Irving Gordon	3 mins 25 secs

Nathaniel Adams Coles (b. March 17, 1919 - d. February 15, 1965) was a singer, actor and television host known professionally as Nat King Cole. He first came to prominence as a leading jazz pianist, and then gained further popularity with his soft baritone voice performing in the big band and jazz genres. By the 1950s he had emerged as a solo performer and scored numerous hits with songs such as; Mona Lisa, Too Young, and Unforgettable. Cole was inducted into the Rock and Roll Hall of Fame in 2000.

---

4 Teresa Brewer
Longing For You

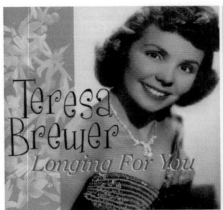

Label:	Written by:	Length:
London Records	Jansen / Dana	2 mins 51 secs

Teresa Brewer (b. 7th May 1931 - d. 17th October 2007) was a singer whose style incorporated country, jazz, R&B, musicals and novelty songs. Nicknamed Miss Music, she was one of the most prolific and popular female singers of the 1950s recording nearly 600 songs. Brewer has a star on the Hollywood Walk of Fame was inducted into the Hit Parade Hall of Fame in 2007.

Vera Lynn
The Homing Waltz

Label:	Written by:	Length:
Decca	Reine / Connor	2 mins 41 secs

Vera Lynn, widely known as the Forces' Sweetheart, is the oldest person to have had a No.1 album in the British charts (aged 92), and became the first centenarian to have a charting album with "Vera Lynn 100" (2017).

Guy Mitchell
There's Always Room At Our House

Label:	Written by:	Length:
Columbia	Bob Merrill	2 mins 43 secs

Guy Mitchell (b. Albert George Cernik, 22nd February 1927 - 1st July 1999) was a pop singer and actor who sold 44 million records and had six million-selling singles during his career. Mitchell's biggest hit, "Singing the Blues", reached the No.1 spot for three (non-consecutive) weeks in the U.K. in early 1957, one of only four singles to rise to No.1 on the chart on three separate occasions.

Jo Stafford
Ay-Round The Corner

Label:	Written by:	Length:
Columbia	Josef Marais	2 mins 34 secs

Jo Elizabeth Stafford (b. 12th November 1917 - d. 16th July 2008) was a traditional pop music singer and occasional actress whose career spanned five decades. Admired for the purity of her voice she originally underwent classical training to become an opera singer before following a career in popular music. By 1955 she had achieved more worldwide record sales than any other female artist.

Mario Lanza
The Loveliest Night Of The Year

Label:	Written by:	Length:
RCA	Aaronson / Webster	3 mins 35 secs

Mario Lanza (b. Alfredo Arnold Cocozza; 31st January 1921 - d. 7th October 1959) was a tenor, actor and Hollywood film star of the late 1940s and the 1950s. Lanza began studying to be a professional singer at the age of 16 and after appearing at the Hollywood Bowl in 1947 signed a seven-year film contract with Louis B. Mayer, the head of Metro-Goldwyn-Mayer, who saw his performance and was impressed by his singing. Success followed and by the time of his death in 1959 he was the most famous tenor in the world.

Rosemary Clooney
Half As Much

Label:	Written by:	Length:
Columbia	Curley Williams	2 mins 45 secs

Rosemary Clooney (b. 23rd May 1928 - d. 29th June 2002) was a singer and actress who came to prominence in 1951 with the song "Come On-A My House". This was followed by a number of other successful pop recordings such as "Botch-A-Me", "Mambo Italiano", "Tenderly", "Half As Much", "Hey There" and "This Ole House". Clooney was awarded the Society of Singers Lifetime Achievement Award in 1998, and received a Grammy Lifetime Achievement Award in 2002.

Jo Stafford
You Belong To Me

Label:	Written by:	Length:
Columbia	Price / King / Stewart	3 mins 14 secs

Jo Stafford's recording of "You Belong To Me" topped the charts in both the United States and United Kingdom; it was the second ever single to top the U.K. Singles Chart after Al Martino's "Here In My Heart". Stafford has been recognised for her work in radio, television, and music with three stars on the Hollywood Walk of Fame.

1952: TOP FILMS

1. **The Greatest Show On Earth** - *Paramount Pictures*
2. **High Noon** - *United Artists*
3. **Singin' In The Rain** - *Metro-Goldwyn-Mayer*
4. **The Quiet Man** - *Republic Pictures*
5. **Ivanhoe** - *Metro-Goldwyn-Mayer*

OSCARS

Best Picture: The Greatest Show On Earth

Most Nominations: High Noon (7), Moulin Rouge (7), The Quiet Man (7)
Most Wins: The Bad And The Beautiful (5)

Shirley Booth, Katherine DeMille (for Anthony Quinn), Cecil B. DeMille & Gloria Grahame.

Best Director: John Ford - *The Quiet Man*

Best Actor: Gary Cooper - *High Noon*
Best Actress: Shirley Booth - *Come Back, Little Sheba*
Best Supporting Actor: Anthony Quinn - *Viva Zapata!*
Best Supporting Actress: Gloria Grahame - *The Bad And The Beautiful*

The 25th Academy Awards, honouring the best in film for 1952, were presented on the 19th March 1953 at the RKO Pantages Theatre in Hollywood, and the NBC International Theatre in New York City.

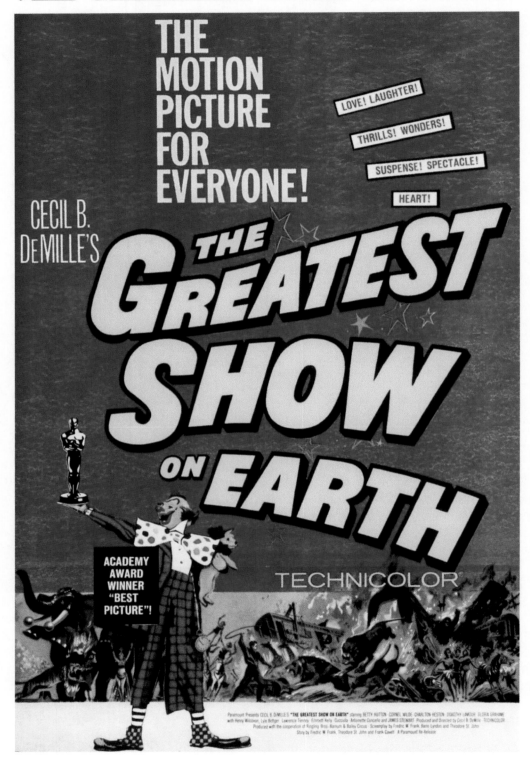

Directed by: Cecil B. DeMille - Runtime: 2h 32m

A dazzling spectacle of life behind the scenes with the Ringling Bros. and Barnum & Bailey Circus, the best three-ring circus in the land.

Starring

Betty Hutton
b. 26th February 1921
d. 12th March 2007
Character:
Holly

Cornel Wilde
b. 13th October 1912
d. 16th October 1989
Character:
The Great Sebastian

Charlton Heston
b. 4th October 1923
d. 5th April 2008
Character:
Brad Braden

Trivia

Goof | When Mickey Mouse and the other Disney characters walk around the ring the band plays the song "It's A Hap-Hap-Happy Day" from Gulliver's Travels (1939), which was released by Paramount, not Disney.

Interesting Facts | Charlton Heston was driving through the Paramount Pictures lot when he spotted Cecil B. DeMille, whom he had never met. Heston waved. DeMille was so impressed by Heston's wave he made inquiries that ultimately led to Heston being cast as Brad in this film. This was only Heston's third film and it skyrocketed him to fame. One fan wrote a letter to DeMille on how much she enjoyed the film and commented, "And I'm surprised how well the circus manager (Heston) worked with the real actors". Heston thought it was one of the best reviews he ever received.

Despite his made-to-order background as a real-life circus acrobat, Burt Lancaster declined the role of The Great Sebastian, a fact Cecil B. DeMille doubly regretted when he learned that Cornel Wilde was afraid of heights. Wilde was game however and ended up performing many of his own stunts on the flying trapeze.

James Stewart plays the entire film in his clown makeup.

Cecil B. DeMille considered Marlene Dietrich and Hedy Lamarr for the lead but ultimately settled on Betty Hutton when the actress sent him an enormous 1,000-dollar floral piece featuring a replica of herself swinging from a trapeze. DeMille accepted her on the condition that she slimmed down her hips.

Quote | *[to Holly, as his blood is being transfused into Brad]*
Sebastian: If he should make love well after this, pay no attention - it will be me.

HIGH NOON

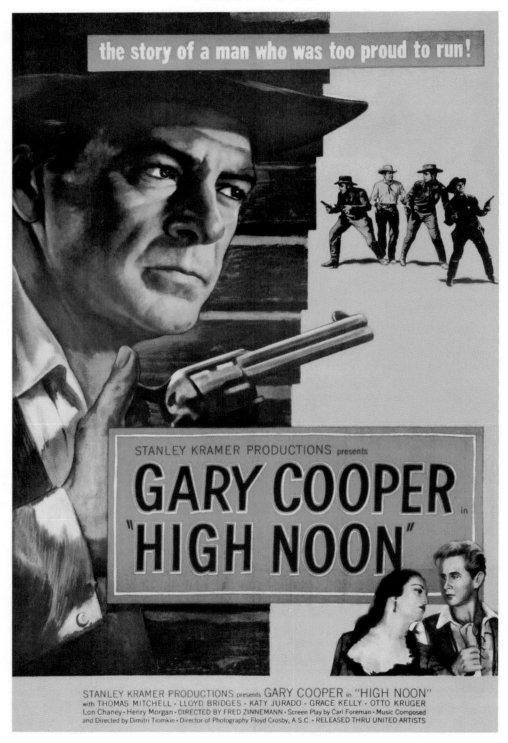

Directed by: Fred Zinnemann - Runtime: 1h 25m

Town Marshal Will Kane must face a gang of deadly killers alone at high noon when Frank Miller, an outlaw he once sent away to be hanged, is due to arrive by train hell-bent on exacting his revenge.

Starring

Gary Cooper
b. 7th May 1901
d. 13th May 1961
Character:
Will Kane

Thomas Mitchell
b. 11th July 1892
d. 17th December 1962
Character:
Jonas Henderson

Lloyd Bridges
b. 15th January 1913
d. 10th March 1998
Character:
Harvey Pell

Trivia

Goofs | In the climactic crane shot, when Kane is alone in the town square, modern-day buildings, high-voltage power lines, and telephone poles are clearly visible in the skyline.

When the mayor makes his speech in church there are children sitting in the pews with the adults. The children then disappear, but return in the next shot.

Interesting Facts | Producer Stanley Kramer first offered the leading role of Will Kane to Gregory Peck, who turned it down because he felt it was too similar to The Gunfighter (1950). Other actors who turned down the role included Charlton Heston, Marlon Brando, Kirk Douglas, Montgomery Clift and Burt Lancaster.

Lee Van Cleef was originally hired to play Deputy Marshal Harvey Pell. However, producer Stanley Kramer decided that his nose was too "hooked", which made him look like a villain, and told him to get it fixed. Van Cleef refused and Lloyd Bridges got the part. Van Cleef was given the smaller role of gunman Jack Colby, one of the Miller gang.

There was some question as to the casting of Gary Cooper since he was 50-years-old and Grace Kelly, playing his wife Amy Fowler Kane, was only 21 (despite this being fairly commonplace for the period in which this film is set). Will Kane was only supposed to be aged around 30.

"The Ballad of High Noon", sung by popular Country Music singer and actor Tex Ritter (also known by its opening lyric, Do Not Forsake Me, O My Darlin') was the first ever Oscar-winning song from a non-musical film.

Quote | **Helen:** You're a good-looking boy, you've big, broad shoulders. But he's a man. And it takes more than big, broad shoulders to make a man.

SINGIN' IN THE RAIN

Directed by: Stanley Donen & Gene Kelly - Runtime: 1h 43m

In 1927 Hollywood a silent film production company and its cast make a difficult transition to sound.

Starring

Gene Kelly
b. 23rd August 1912
d. 2nd February 1996
Character:
Don Lockwood

Donald O'Connor
b. 28th August 1925
d. 27th September 2003
Character:
Cosmo Brown

Debbie Reynolds
b. 1st April 1932
d. 28th December 2016
Character:
Kathy Selden

Trivia

Goofs

As Kathy takes Don to Sunset and Camden, 1950s-era cars can be seen passing in the background (the film is set in 1927).

At the end of "Beautiful Girl" all the models gather, but one of them loses her "Swim Suit Girl" pose as she walks down the steps, almost tripping.

Interesting Facts

Debbie Reynolds remarked many years later that making this film and surviving childbirth were the two hardest things she'd ever had to do. The filming experience was particularly unpleasant due to her harsh treatment by perfectionist Gene Kelly. Decades later, Kelly expressed remorse about his behaviour: "I wasn't nice to Debbie. It's a wonder she still speaks to me".

The "Broadway Ballet" sequence took a month to rehearse, two weeks to shoot, and cost $600,000, almost a fifth of the overall budget.

Only 19 when cast to play the film, Debbie Reynolds lived with her parents and commuted to the set. She had to wake up at 4:00 a.m. and ride three different buses to the studio; sometimes, to avoid the commute, she would just sleep on the set.

In 2007 the American Film Institute ranked this as the 5th Greatest Movie of All Time.

Quotes

[Don Lockwood is being mobbed by several fans on the street]
Don Lockwood: *[desperately]* Hey, Cos! Do something! Call me a cab!
Cosmo Brown: OK, you're a cab.
Don Lockwood: *[unimpressed]* Thanks a lot!

Audience Member: Did somebody get paid for writing that dialog?

THE QUIET MAN

Directed by: John Ford - Runtime: 2h 9m

Retired American boxer Sean Thornton returns to the village of his birth in Ireland where he falls for a spirited redhead whose brother is contemptuous of their union.

Starring

John Wayne
b. 26th May 1907
d. 11th June 1979
Character:
Sean Thornton

Maureen O'Hara
b. 17th August 1920
d. 24th October 2015
Character:
Mary Kate Danaher

Barry Fitzgerald
b. 10th March 1888
d. 14th January 1961
Character:
Michaleen Oge Flynn

Trivia

Goofs John Wayne's wedding ring is visible before he even meets Mary Kate Danniher. It is most clearly seen while he is remembering his mother's words before introducing himself to Michaleen.

During the fight, the last time Sean gets the bucket of water thrown on him, we hear him say, "Thanks", but his lips never move.

Interesting Facts In the scene where John Wayne discovers Maureen O'Hara in his cottage, the wind whipped her hair so ferociously around her face she kept squinting. John Ford screamed at her in the strongest language to open her eyes. O'Hara quipped, "What would a bald-headed son of a bitch know about hair lashing across his eyeballs".

John Wayne was disappointed by the unconvincing studio sets that were used for exterior scenes.

"The Quiet Man" was a significant departure for Republic Pictures which specialised in low-budget westerns, comedies and war pictures. It was the company's first and only film to receive an Oscar nomination for Best Picture.

This film won John Ford an unprecedented fourth Best Director Academy Award. He had won previously for The Informer (1935), The Grapes of Wrath (1940) and How Green Was My Valley (1941).

Quotes **Father Peter Lonergan, Narrator:** Ah, yes... I knew your people, Sean. Your grandfather; he died in Australia, in a penal colony. And your father, he was a good man too.

"Red Will" Danaher: He'll regret it till his dying day, if ever he lives that long.

SPORTING WINNERS

FIVE NATIONS RUGBY
WALES

Position	Nation	Played	Won	Draw	Lost	For	Against	+/-	Points
1	**Wales**	**4**	**4**	**0**	**0**	**42**	**14**	**+28**	**8**
2	England	4	3	0	1	34	14	+20	6
3	Ireland	4	2	0	2	26	33	-7	4
4	France	4	1	0	3	29	37	-8	2
5	Scotland	4	0	0	4	22	55	-33	0

The 1952 and twenty-third series of the rugby union Five Nations Championship saw ten matches played between the 12th January and the 5th April. Including the previous incarnations as the Home Nations and Five Nations, this was the fifty-eighth series of the northern hemisphere rugby union championship. The competition saw Wales win their 12th title and 9th Triple Crown.

Date	Team		Score	Team		Location
12-01-1952	Scotland		11-13	France		Edinburgh
19-01-1952	England		6-8	Wales		London
26-01-1952	France		8-11	Ireland		Paris
02-02-1952	Wales		11-0	Scotland		Cardiff
23-02-1952	Ireland		12-8	Scotland		Dublin
08-03-1952	Ireland		3-14	Wales		Dublin
15-03-1952	Scotland		3-19	England		Edinburgh
22-03-1952	Wales		9-5	France		Swansea
29-03-1952	England		3-0	Ireland		London
05-04-1952	France		3-6	England		Paris

CALCUTTA CUP

SCOTLAND 3-19 ENGLAND

The Calcutta Cup was first awarded in 1879 and is the rugby union trophy awarded to the winner of the match (currently played as part of the Six Nations Championship) between England and Scotland. The Cup was presented to the Rugby Football Union after the Calcutta Football Club in India disbanded in 1878; it is made from melted down silver rupees withdrawn from the club's funds.

BRITISH GRAND PRIX

Piero Taruffi (left) and Alberto Ascari celebrate their triumph in the 1952 British Grand Prix.

The 1952 British Grand Prix was held at Silverstone on the 19th July and was won by Alberto Ascari over 85 laps of the 2.927-mile circuit. It was race 5 of 8 in the 1952 World Championship of Drivers, in which each Grand Prix was run to Formula Two rules rather than the Formula One regulations normally used.

Pos.	Country	Driver	Car
1	**Italy**	**Alberto Ascari**	**Ferrari**
2	Italy	Piero Taruffi	Ferrari
3	United Kingdom	Mike Hawthorn	Cooper-Bristol

NB: The Silverstone circuit is built on the site of the World War II Royal Air Force bomber station, RAF Silverstone; Silverstone first hosted the British Grand Prix in 1948.

1952 GRAND PRIX SEASON

Date	Race	Circuit	Winning Driver	Constructor
18-05	Swiss GP	Bremgarten	Piero Taruffi	Ferrari
30-05	Indy 500	Indianapolis	Troy Ruttman	Kuzma-Offenhauser
22-06	Belgian GP	Spa	Alberto Ascari	Ferrari
06-07	French GP	Rouen-Les-Essarts	Alberto Ascari	Ferrari
19-07	British GP	Silverstone	Alberto Ascari	Ferrari
03-08	German GP	Nürburgring	Alberto Ascari	Ferrari
17-08	Dutch GP	Zandvoort	Alberto Ascari	Ferrari
07-09	Italian GP	Monza	Alberto Ascari	Ferrari

The 1952 Grand Prix season was dominated by Ferrari whose drivers who took the top three positions in the Championship; 1st Alberto Ascari (36 points), 2nd Giuseppe Farina (25 points), and 3rd Piero Taruffi (24 points).

GRAND NATIONAL - TEAL

The 1952 Grand National was the 106th renewal of this world famous horse race and took place at Aintree Racecourse near Liverpool on the 5th April. The winning horse was Teal who was trained by Neville Crump and ridden by Irish jockey Arthur Thompson.

Of the 47 runners only 10 horses actually completed the course; 25 fell, 4 refused, 3 pulled up, 3 were brought down, and 2 unseated their riders; all but one horse, Skouras, returned safely to the stables afterwards. *Photo: Teal (left) takes the final fence at Aintree before going on to win the 1952 Grand National.*

	Horse	Jockey	Age	Weight	Odds
1st	**Teal**	**Arthur Thompson**	**10**	**10st-12lb**	**100/7**
2nd	Legal Joy	Michael Scudamore	9	10st-4lb	100/6
3rd	Wot No Sun	David Dick	10	11st-7lb	33/1

EPSOM DERBY - TULYAR

The Derby Stakes is Britain's richest horse race and the most prestigious of the country's five Classics. First run in 1780 this Group 1 flat horse race is open to 3-year-old thoroughbred colts and fillies. The race takes place at Epsom Downs in Surrey over a distance of one mile, four furlongs and 10 yards (2,423 metres) and is scheduled for early June each year. The 1952 Derby was won by jockey Charlie Smirke aboard Tulyar.

Photo: Irish-bred, British-trained Thoroughbred racehorse and sire Tulyar (1949-1972) after winning the 1952 Epsom Derby. Tulyar was owned by Sir Sultan Mahomed Shah, Aga Khan III, and trained by Marcus Marsh.

FOOTBALL LEAGUE CHAMPIONS

England

Pos.	Team	W	D	L	F	A	Pts.
1	**Manchester United**	**23**	**11**	**8**	**95**	**52**	**57**
2	Tottenham Hotspur	22	9	11	76	51	53
3	Arsenal	21	11	10	80	61	53
4	Portsmouth	20	8	14	68	58	48
5	Bolton Wanderers	19	10	13	65	61	48

Scotland

Pos.	Team	W	D	L	F	A	Pts.
1	**Hibernian**	**20**	**5**	**5**	**92**	**36**	**45**
2	Rangers	16	9	5	61	31	41
3	East Fife	17	3	10	71	49	37
4	Heart of Midlothian	14	7	9	69	53	35
5	Raith Rovers	14	5	11	43	42	33

FA CUP WINNERS - NEWCASTLE UNITED

Newcastle United   1-0   Arsenal

The 1952 FA Cup Final took place on the 3rd May at Wembley Stadium in front of 100,000 fans. Newcastle United won the match to take the Cup for the fifth time, and the second year in succession; George Robledo scored the games' only goal. *Photo: Newcastle United's captain Joe Harvey is held aloft after their victory over Arsenal in the FA Cup final.*

Snooker - Horace Lindrum

Horace Lindrum 94-49 Clark McConachy

The 1952 World Snooker Championship was held at Houldsworth Hall in Manchester between the 25th February and 8th March. There were only two entrants, Australian Horace Lindrum and New Zealander Clark McConachy, following a dispute between the governing body and the players' association. *Photo: Horace Lindrum in London circa 1952.*

Golf - Open Championship - Bobby Locke

The 1952 Open Championship was the 81st to be played and was held between the 9th and 11th July at Royal Lytham & St Annes Golf Club in Lytham St Annes, Lancashire. South African Bobby Locke won the third of his four Claret Jugs (one stroke ahead of runner-up Peter Thomson) to take the £300 winners share of the £1,700 prize fund.

WIMBLEDON

Photos: 1952 Wimbledon Singles Champions Frank Sedgman and Maureen Connolly.

Men's Singles Champion - Frank Sedgman - Australia
Ladies Singles Champion - Maureen Connolly - United States

The 1952 Wimbledon Championships was the 66th staging of tournament and took place on the outdoor grass courts at the All England Lawn Tennis and Croquet Club in Wimbledon, London. It ran from the 23rd June until the 5th July and was the third Grand Slam tennis event of 1952.

Men's Singles Final

Country	Player	Set 1	Set 2	Set 3	Set 4
Australia	Frank Sedgman	4	6	6	6
Egypt	Jaroslav Drobný	6	2	3	2

Women's Singles Final

Country	Player	Set 1	Set 2
United States	Maureen Connolly	7	6
United States	Louise Brough	5	3

Men's Doubles Final

Country	Players	Set 1	Set 2	Set 3
Australia	Ken McGregor / Frank Sedgman	6	7	6
United States / South Africa	Vic Seixas / Eric Sturgess	3	5	4

Women's Doubles Final

Country	Players	Set 1	Set 2
United States	Shirley Fry / Doris Hart	8	6
United States	Louise Brough / Maureen Connolly	6	3

Mixed Doubles Final

Country	Players	Set 1	Set 2	Set 3
Australia / United States	Frank Sedgman / Doris Hart	4	6	6
Argentina / Australia	Enrique Morea / Thelma Long	6	3	4

County Championship Cricket - Surrey

1952 saw the fifty-third officially organised running of the County Championship. It ran from the 3rd May to the 2nd September and was the beginning of Surrey's period of dominance as they won the first of seven successive County Championships.

Pos.	Team	Pld.	W	L	D	Tied	ND	Pts.
1	**Surrey**	**28**	**20**	**3**	**5**	**0**	**0**	**256**
2	Yorkshire	28	17	2	8	0	1	224
3	Lancashire	28	12	3	11	1	1	188
4	Derbyshire	28	11	8	9	0	0	164
5	Middlesex	28	11	12	4	0	1	136
6	Leicestershire	28	9	9	9	0	1	132
7	Glamorgan	28	8	7	13	0	0	130

Test Series
England 3-0 India

1st Test | Headingley, 5th - 9th June - Result: England win by 7 wickets

Innings	Team	Score	Overs	Team	Score	Overs
1st Innings	India	293	126.3	England	334	165.2
2nd Innings	India	165	67	England	128/3	55

2nd Test | Lord's, 19th - 24th June - Result: England win by 8 wickets

Innings	Team	Score	Overs	Team	Score	Overs
1st Innings	India	235	94.3	England	537	206.4
2nd Innings	India	378	122	England	79/2	49.2

3rd Test | Old Trafford, 17th - 19th July - Result: England win by an innings & 207 runs

Innings	Team	Score	Overs	Team	Score	Overs
1st Innings	England	347/9 (d)	144	India	58	21.4
2nd Innings	England	-	-	India	82	36.3

4th Test | The Oval, 14th - 19th August - Result: Match drawn

Innings	Team	Score	Overs	Team	Score	Overs
1st Innings	England	326/6 (d)	154	India	98	38.5
2nd Innings	England	-	-	India	-	-

THE COST OF LIVING

Sweet way to go gay !

ONLY 3ᵈ A PACKET

Handily packed, delicious to eat, SPANGLES are the fruitiest sweet!   *Made by MARS*

Comparison Chart

	1952	1952 (+ Inflation)	2021	% Change
3 Bedroom House	£2,650	£83,997	£235,243	+180.1%
Weekly Income	£5.8s.1d	£171.30	£621	+262.5%
Pint Of Beer	10d	£1.32	£3.94	+198.5%
Cheese (lb)	2s.5d	£3.83	£3.04	-20.6%
Bacon (lb)	2s.6d	£3.96	£3.20	-19.2%
The Beano	2d	26p	£2.75	+961.5%

At Wembley..

....or at Twickenham

...or wherever fine cigarettes are appreciated...smokers prefer

THE BEST CIGARETTES IN THE WORLD

STATE EXPRESS 555

12

The House of STATE EXPRESS 210 PICCADILLY. LONDON. W.I.

THIS IS *IT* CHAPS!
THE "TRUFLITE" THROWING KNIFE

A perfectly balanced Throwing Knife, 7½ in. long from the tip of its hand-ground, mirror-polished, beautifully engraved Sheffield steel blade, to the top of its unbreakable handle; complete with leather sheath, target and instructions: 9/8; Junior "Truflite" (5⅞ in.): 7/10; "SCOUT'S SPECIAL" 8 in. Sheath Knife: 5/4; Super Quality Hunting Knives, 6 in.: 9/4; 8 in. : 13/4; 9 in. : 18/4; all complete with leather sheaths. **DON'T MISS THEM!**

Post and pkg. on each order, 8d. extra.

Robin's
MAIL ORDER SERVICE

(DEPT. M552), 100, EAST ST., LONDON S.E.17

Clothes Prices

Women's Clothing

Key Fashions Luxury Corduroy Coat	£3.19s.11d
Anthony Warren Tailored Jacket	£1.9s.6d
Ian Peters Rayon Bolero	18s.6d
Marilyn Modes Pure Wool Dress	£1.6s.6d
Valuwear Outsize Satin Dress	£1.4s.11d
Delinont Winter Frock	19s.11d
Bond Street Fashions Sundress	7s.6d
American Style Rayon Shantung Shirt	8s.11d
Supreme Fashion Tweed Skirt	£1.2s.6d
Faerie Fashions Pencil Slim Gaberdine Skirt	19s.11d
Fenwick Dressing Gown	4½gns
Ambrose Wilson Elite Corselette	£1.5s
Queensway All Leather Court Shoes	£1.9s
Edward Bros. Foam Rubber Sole Slippers	12s

Men's Clothing

American Type Army Jacket	£5
Windguard Waterproof Suedette Jacket	£1.9s.6d
Peter Grant Made To Measure Suit	£10.10s
Riviera Styled Black Jeans	£1.15s.6d
Brinksway Trousers	13s.11d
Vince Continental Swimming Briefs	16s.6d
RAF / Naval Pattern Shoes	£1.2s.6d

Various Other Items & Their Cost

1952 Ford Consul (inc. 66% purchase tax)	£1,190
1950 Hillman Minx Saloon Car	£1,095
1949 Jaguar 3½ Litre Mk V Car	£1,995
1949 Austin A40 Saloon Car	£1,025
Lucas Fog Lamp	£4.12s.6d
Reconditioned Hercules Bicycle	£4.10s
BEA London To Nice Return Flights	£25
Holiday To Malta (15 days including flight)	82gns
Cruft's Dog Show Admission	6s
Raymond Gas Cooker	60gns
GEC Television & Radio	69gns
DER Television Rental (per week)	15s.9d
Hoover Vacuum Cleaner (refurbished)	£6.15s
35mm Strip Projector (battery model)	£1.7s.6d
Terry Anglepoise Lamp	£4.19s.6d
Walnut Dining Suite	34gns
3-Piece Suite	25gns
Oak 4ft Wardrobe	£16
Axminster Carpet (9ft x 7ft 6in)	£14
Hillman Sewing Machine Motor	£6.18s
J. G. Graves 20 Piece Crockery Set	18s.6d
Aga Iron	£1.17s.6d
Hand Carved Cuckoo Clock	£1.9s.6d
Goya Perfumed Cologne	3s.6d
Boots Hot Water Bottle	4s.11d
Sanderson Indoor Play Tent	£1.3s.6d
Betty American Type Walking Doll	£1.19s.6d
20in Walking, Sitting & Talking Doll	5s
Giant Growling Teddy Bear	8s
Hand Sewn Leather Football	17s.6d
Bread Loaf	7½d
Lucozade	2s.6d
Odo-Ro-No Antiperspirant & Deodorant (jar)	1s.6d
Brylcreem (tube)	2s.6d
Phillips' Dental Magnesia Toothpaste	1s.6d
Woodward's Gripe Water	1s.9d
Milk Of Magnesia Tablets (150)	4s.11d
Beecham's Powders (2)	5½d
Lixen Laxative Lozenges (bottle)	2s.6d
Gordons Gin	£1.13s.9d
Real Tesoro Sherry	20s
Burgoyne's Tintara Wine (flagon)	13s
Whiteway's Ruby/White Wine	5s.9d
The Three Castles Cigarettes (20)	3s.11d
Pigskin Cigarette Case	£5.5s
Daily Mirror Newspaper	1½d
Postage Stamp	2½d

Lambretta

Soon all the World and his wife will be travelling cheaply and in comfort on this wonderful machine.

140 M.P.G.

Shaft Drive—
no messy chains.

Complete protection
from road dust.

Side cars available

*Visit your nearest Agent for
demonstration or write to:—*

LAMBRETTA CONCESSIONAIRES LTD.

Head Office: 64 High St., Epsom, Surrey. 'Phone: Epsom 3435/6
Service and Spares: 213 The Broadway, Wimbledon, S.W.19. 'Phone: Liberty 1390

Lambretta MODERN TRANSPORT

Money Conversion Table

Pounds / Shillings / Pence 1952 'Old Money'		Decimal Value	Value 2021 (Rounded)
Farthing	¼d	0.1p	3p
Half Penny	½d	0.21p	7p
Penny	1d	0.42p	13p
Threepence	3d	1.25p	40p
Sixpence	6d	2.5p	79p
Shilling	1s	5p	£1.58
Florin	2s	10p	£3.17
Half Crown	2s.6d	12.5p	£3.96
Crown	5s	25p	£7.92
Ten Shillings	10s	50p	£15.85
Pound	20s	£1	£31.70
Guinea	21s	£1.05	£33.28
Five Pounds	£5	£5	£158.49
Ten Pounds	£10	£10	£316.97

The Toucans aren't loquacious birds —
Their beaks are just too big for words.
Guinness, they say, is good for you;
So why not see what toucan do?

This is the Gin
for every occasion and every taste

SPECIAL DRY GIN
The gin of incomparable quality—'the heart of a good cocktail'. Bottle 33/9d. ½ bottle 17/7d. ¼ bottle 9/2d. Miniature 3/7d. U.K. only.

ORANGE GIN AND LEMON GIN
Delicious on its own, with tonic water or a splash of soda. Bottle 32/-. ½ bottle 16/9. Miniature 3/5d. U.K. only.

'SHAKER' COCKTAILS
'There's no comparison'—seven appetising varieties mixed by experts and ready to serve from shaker bottles. Bottle 21/-. ½ bottle 11/3d. Miniature 2/5d. U.K. only.

Gordon's
Stands Supreme

Printed in Great Britain
by Amazon